MONK SEAL HIDEAWAY

Diane Ackerman

MONK SEAL HIDEAWAY

photographs by Bill Curtsinger

Crown Publishers, Inc., New York

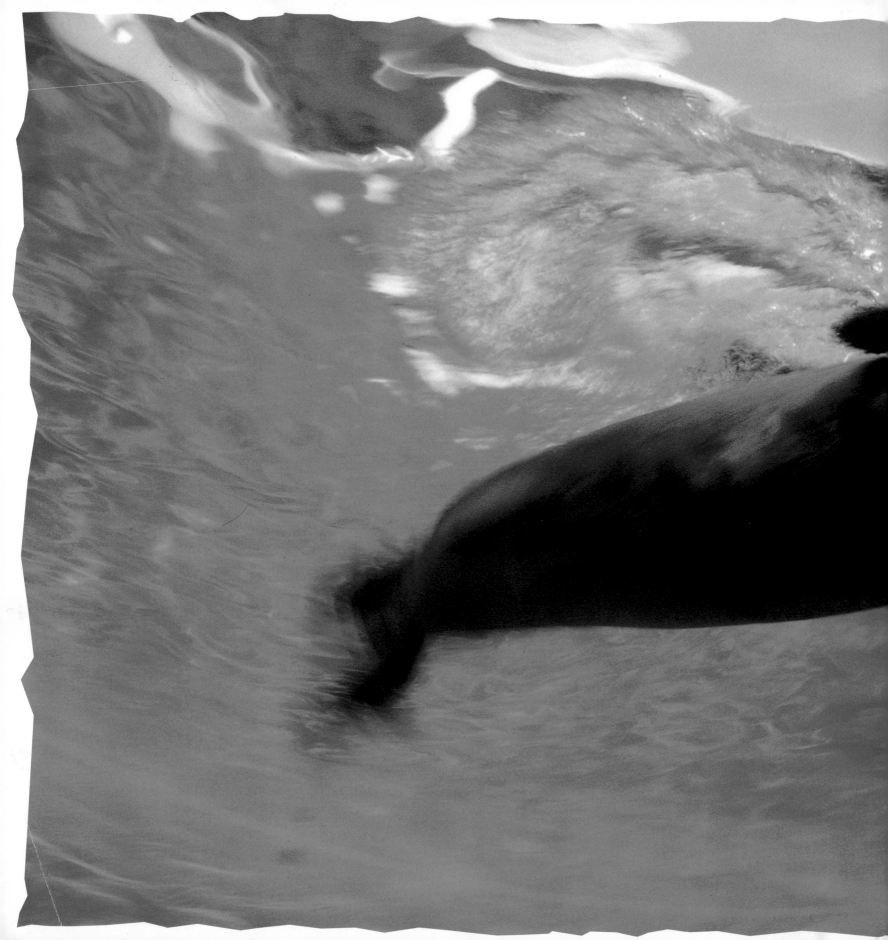

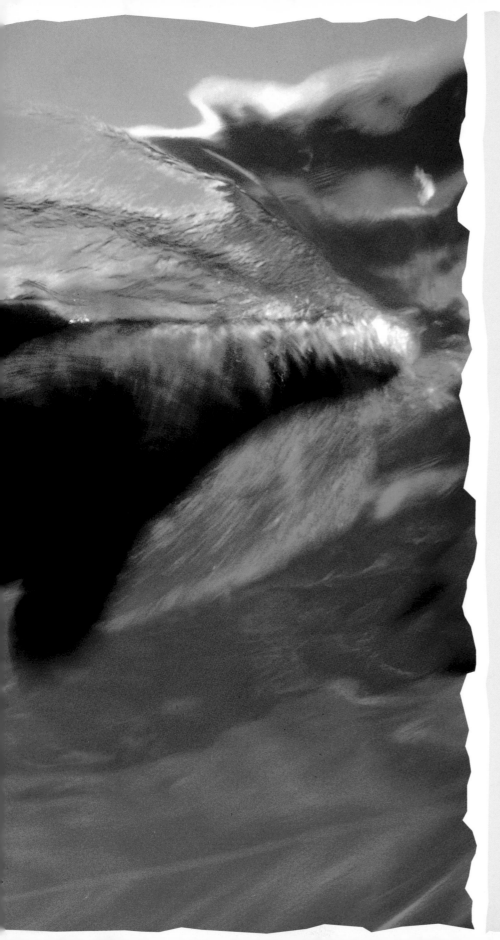

One sleepy summer day, I lay on a cushion behind my house, basking in the sun like any alligator, tarantula, or cocker spaniel. The bees were kazooing in the lavender bed. The squirrels were hot-rodding up and down the hickory trees. The rabbits were jousting on the lawn. (They looked like furry knights.) Every now and then, a groundhog waddled across the grass and dug up one of my prize flowers. Dragonflies flew loops and rolls overhead. A tiny lizard did push-ups on a fence post. And a bossy wren sat on a branch, near a birdhouse in which her nearly naked chicks peeped, and she pestered the whole wide world. In short, it was a perfect summer day.

I was daydreaming about a mysterious animal I had once heard of that lived far away in a bright blue kingdom of sand and ocean. Its name is "monk seal," and it is sometimes also called a "living fossil," because it is the most ancient of all seals (15 million years old).

"The most ancient seal. What does the ancient look like, anyway?" I thought. "Like a dinosaur? Like a wrinkled old man?"

At the library, I found a photograph of a monk seal. It had a round head covered in silvery fur, with black buttonhook-shaped eyes, a snout on which nostrils open like quotation marks, tiny tab-shaped ears, a spray of cat's whiskers, and many double chins. It seemed to look young and unformed, with a round puppyish face. Is that what the ancient looks like—all soft lines and curves like the planet itself? But the write-up told me nothing about the real animals—how they looked, sounded, moved through the water and across the sand, found mates, raised their young. This wouldn't do at all. I had no choice but to go and see monk seals for myself.

So a few months later, I flew to Hawaii with a photographer friend, Bill. There Bill and I joined Gil, a man who studies monk seals, and the three of us rented a small plane and flew northwest to a horseshoe-shaped spill of islands and sand spits where the last Hawaiian monk seals live. Very few are left—only about 1,500. Soon they may go extinct like the dinosaurs, and we will only read about them in books.

TERN ISLAND

TRIG ISLAND

SKATE ISLAND

WHALE ISLAND

SHARK ISLAND

ROUND ISLAND
MULLET ISLAND

FRENCH FRIGATE SHOALS

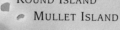
BARE ISLAND

EAST ISLAND

GIN ISLAND

LITTLE GIN
ISLAND

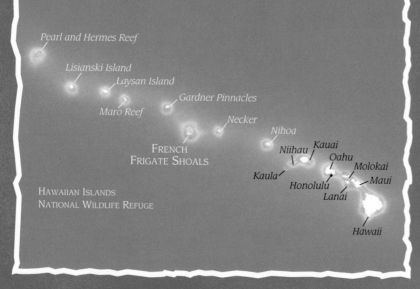

HAWAIIAN ISLANDS

Pearl and Hermes Reef

Lisianski Island

Laysan Island

Gardner Pinnacles

Maro Reef

Necker

Nihoa

FRENCH
FRIGATE SHOALS

Niihau

Kauai

Oahu

Molokai

Maui

Kaula

Honolulu

Lanai

HAWAIIAN ISLANDS
NATIONAL WILDLIFE REFUGE

Hawaii

DISAPPEARING ISLAND

French Frigate Shoals is a group of 12 small islands in the Pacific Ocean, 450 miles northwest of Hawaii. They are part of the Hawaiian Islands National Wildlife Refuge.

Monk seals used to live in other places around the world, in the Mediterranean and the Caribbean seas. The last recorded Caribbean monk seal was spotted as recently as 1952. I was four years old then, growing up in a small town in Illinois, playing in the plum orchard across from my house, learning to count. I didn't know that an animal that had survived for 15 million years was, at that moment,

becoming extinct. Nor that most people would only see monk seals flattened in a textbook or stuffed in a museum. The few that live near Hawaii survive because they've found a remote hiding place.

Suddenly, Tern Island materialized

beneath us. Coming in to land, our pilots put on white crash helmets, in case a bird hit the windshield and shattered it. We laughed. How could there be that many birds? But there were huge clouds of birds! When the pilot lined up with a broad coral runway and cut the engines, we saw great flocks of frigate birds, boobies, and terns burst like flak into the air all around us. As we touched down, a second barrage of birds flew up—brown noddies, this time, and shearwaters and plovers. And in a cyclone of birds, we came to rest at last in front of a long barracks, outside of which a plaque read: TERN ISLAND, FRENCH FRIGATE SHOALS. POPULATION 4.

We all had jobs to do. Gil and I were going to tag this year's seal pups and check the general health of the adults. Bill was going to photograph monk seals. We climbed into a small motorboat and set out for a small slipper-shaped island six miles away. After a wave-leaping ride of forty minutes, we saw a bright coin on the horizon sliding closer and closer.

Composed entirely of coarse coral sand and pulverized shells, East Island wasn't very large, and it didn't rise more than eight or ten feet above sea level. Actually, it looked more like a tablecloth than an island, and a brisk storm could dash waves right over it.

Masked boobies, sooty terns, and Laysan albatrosses flew out to greet us as we picked our way among the coral, at last settling for a spot on the quieter side of the island. Bill dropped one anchor in the ocean, and I slid over the side with a second anchor, ran up the beach, and planted its steel claws in a small dune.

Wading through the warm, pale water, we carried buckets and gear on our heads like jungle porters, and left them in a heap on shore. The sun felt hot as a branding iron on our exposed skin. There was no shade, and the coral sand, like millions of small, perfectly white teeth, reflected all of the sun's fury.

Frigate bird

Fairy tern

Suddenly I caught sight of my first monk seal! Browner than I imagined and molting in patches, the large seal looked a little like an old horsehair couch someone left by the curb. Its belly glowed a creamy beige. Lying placidly with its muzzle half-buried in sand, the seal snoozed as incoming waves swirled around its face, sudsing its whiskers. Because breathing is so regular and automatic for us, we forget that other animals use air on different schedules. Seals need to hold their breath long enough to swim and hunt under water. After the monk seal inhaled and exhaled three times in a row, its chest stayed motionless for ten minutes. Then, lifting its heavy head, it sneezed loudly with a wild twisting of the neck, and settled back on the sand with a loud *harrumph*. Monk seals suffer from nose mites—tiny insects even smaller than fleas—which give them terrible sinus problems. Although they can use their webbed front flippers to scratch at the face and mouth, they can't reach the mites very well. So they sneeze often, loudly, and wetly.

Strolling past a low dune, we came upon six large seals lying in parallel in the sand. Then a smaller seal, sleeping in the middle of the island, took a few breaths, woke up, and steam-shoveled its way closer to the water, digging a trench as it went.

After a long night of searching for food, monk seals bask in the severe heat of the day. They like to dig down to a cool, damp layer of sand. In many places we found "tractor paths" left by monk seals that had dragged themselves to the water.

▼ *Monk seal pup*

Time to start tagging. Gil bent his knees, rounded his shoulders, and sneaked up close to the sleeping monk seals, checking to see if any were pups in need of flipper tags. The information researchers get from tagging helps them study the habits and movements of the animals, and that makes protecting them easier. Turning back toward me, Gil pointed to a small dark seal right at the end of the row. Opening the white tagging bucket, I removed a leather belt-punch, two fraying kneepads, paper and pencil, a tape measure, and two numbered yellow plastic flipper tags. I practiced opening and closing the tags a few times, slid on the kneepads, and coiled up the tape measure, which I tucked under my bathing suit so I could grab it fast.

Okay, I nodded to Gil, and crept up behind him. Stealthy and alert, he hunkered down and sneaked right up behind the seal, climbed onto its back and gripped its cheeks in both hands. Waking with a loud gargling *Baah!*, the seal began rolling and

squirming as I rushed in, fell to my knees behind its tail, and tried to catch the twin flippers flailing around in such confusion that it was hard to tell left from right. I

grabbed one flipper out of midair and pressed it flat on the sand while the other smacked my face.

"How ya doin'?" Gil called from in front. Straddling the seal's back, he was not actually sitting on it but corraling it with his long legs. Gripping its double chins, he held its sharp teeth away from him, which also kept the seal belly-down.

"At the tags," I called back just as both flippers sailed up and punched me under the chin, then slapped me full face from left to right, knocking me back off my knees. I crawled into place again, amazed by the sucker punch of the flippers. Each can open to a foot wide or close up as tight as a baseball bat. But both are driven by a single powerful muscle at the base of the tail, a muscle as thick as a human arm. Now the flippers clapped and rolled like someone packing a snowball, and it was hard to tell which was which. I grabbed one, flattened it on the sand, and finally attached the tag.

"One done!" I called to Gil. Sweat had begun pouring down my face, carrying sand with it. The seal's wet fur smelled chalky sweet. We had interrupted its sleep, and it complained in a low steady gargle as I pulled the remaining tag from my waistband and attached it. Only minutes were passing, but they felt long and hot.

"Two done!" I called to Gil.

▼ *Gray reef and tiger sharks are monk seals' main natural enemy. They strike when seals are feeding at night. This pup was attacked, and although Gil is working to save it, it probably will not survive.*

Left: *The rear flippers of a monk seal pup with plastic yellow tags. The letter tells what year the pup was tagged, the color indicates the location, and the number identifies the individual seal.* **Right:** *The monk seal's powerful front flipper.*

The Hawaiian monk seal lives for approximately 30 years and can reach nine feet in length. Females can weigh up to 550 lbs., while the smaller males weigh up to 375 lbs.

Next we measured the monk seal. Yanking the tape measure free, I slid one end under Gil's rump and into his right hand so that he could pull it to the tip of the seal's nose; I pulled the other end to the tip of the tail. That task done, I took the tape measure and moved to the right side of the seal, which eyed me suspiciously. What big black eyes and long, stiff whiskers. It had a cleft in its nose just as a cat does or a llama, and a soft cream-colored overbite. *BAAAH!* Its gargle seemed to come from a great distance and echo all over the island.

"Under the flippers!" Gil called to me.

Watching out for the teeth, I slid the tape measure under the seal's chin, under the chest, and over the back just behind the flippers.

"That's it," Gil said, climbing off. The seal rolled onto one side, facing us, and pawed the air with a flipper. As it did, we saw four tiny nipples halfway down its fawn-colored belly, and a slit right under the tail. Female. A precious pup. There aren't many female

monk seals left, so each one must be carefully watched and protected. Moving to a polite distance, we saw the newly tagged pup roll over in the sand and return to basking as if nothing very special had happened. Gil was pleased to find a female pup so fat and healthy and full of spunk.

◀ *Two monk seals sleep next to a pile of fishing nets that have washed ashore. Lost fishing nets are a leading cause of death among Hawaiian monk seals. The seals become entangled in them and cannot come to the surface to breathe.*

From a distance, East Island had appeared flat as a sand dollar, but its gentle dunes rise high enough to hide sleeping monk seals. As we continued our walk, we chanced upon many more of them dozing peacefully in the surf, always facing out to sea. Were they watching for something, I wondered? Or did they just relish the feel of the waves lapping at the whiskers, swirling around the muzzle, sudsing the nose?

Unlike other seals, which like to rub shoulders and lie all over and around each other in a big, loud party of barking and flopping, monk seals are loners. Lying in parallel on the beach, they keep their distance from one another. On this day, the seals occupied all the beaches. But in the spring, the mothers nurse their babies on the south side of the island, where shallow waters are just right for play and they're unlikely to bump into the ten-foot-long tiger sharks that patrol the water around the rest of the island, on the lookout for pups or birds.

Waiting in the shallows, a mother called to her snoozy pup, and the baby *baah*ed back in a slightly higher voice, then waddled into the water and darted to her. Monk seals make many sounds—from stuttering grunts to high-pitched foghorns. A large male monk seal lifted its head, cocked an eye at us, snuffled, put its head back on the damp sand, and closed its eyes in slumber.

▲ This monk seal pup has a tag on its tail.

◄ A monk seal pup under water shows its streamlined shape and its powerful tail and flippers.

Once, when I went wading to cool off, a pup paddled toward me. I sat down up to my shoulders in the water as it swam in close, twitching its nose and having a good look-see. For long seconds, it stared hard at me. Casting a few more glances over its shoulder, it turned to grab an empty bottle bobbing beside it in the water. It tossed  the bottle in the air, nudged it with its nose, and played with it like a bathtub toy.

Popping its head up in the periscope-like way that seals do, the pup watched me, then had a rollicking good sneeze. Pups are troubled by nose mites, just as adults are, but they have higher voices than adults, and when they sneeze, they sound like cellophane tearing. Tiring of the bottle, the pup swam toward me again, this time straight across our boat's anchor line, which it lay on top of, paddle-flailing in a splashy commotion of flippers, until it got bored at last and swam away.

For forty days, a mother will tend her pup without eating. During that time, the pup will gain 175 pounds, but the mother will lose 350 pounds. At last, scrawny and famished, she'll go out on a feeding binge, then find a mate. Next she'll spend seven to ten days molting, during which time she'll fast once more.

Female monk seals practice "fostering." If two mothers are nursing pups and the pups briefly stray, it's likely that the mothers will exchange pups. They either can't tell whose pup is whose or they don't care.

At first glance, this may seem helpful. If there are few members of a population, isn't it smart for everyone to look after the young? But, unfortunately, mother monk seals can't continue nursing forever. When a swap takes place, a younger pup may end up with a mother that has been nursing for some time and not have enough milk left to raise the young pup. Weaned too soon, the undersize pup will not be able to feed itself.

Bobbing in the ocean, a mother monk *baah*ed to her black pup, which *baah*ed

back. On land, an adult seal drags itself with great effort, or ripple-gallops like a 400-pound slug. But the water sets it free to swivel and race. It can grow to nine feet long, and its torpedo-shaped body can outmaneuver a shark. What feeding monk seals usually do is dive down 25 to 400 feet on the reef, find a spiny lobster, slap it on the surface to break it, then eat just the succulent tail. Their diet also includes eels, squid, octopi, and some reef fishes.

▲ *A female monk seal nursing a pup.*

When you look at a napping monk seal, it's like looking at a landscape. There is a graceful, hilly rise and fall to their outline, a soft geography. Sometimes they molt and shed all their old fur, which is slowly replaced by new fur. At molting time, they look as if they were putting on their old trousers when they got tired and lay down to rest halfway through. When a monk seal's whiskers dry, they curl up into a mustache; when they get wet, they straighten out. Older monk seals develop gray whiskers. Sometimes they raise their tail flippers higher than the rest of their

them when they sleep. On an incline, they find it easiest to move by first curling their tail around, making a crescent of their body, and then shifting their weight until they're off balance, rolling downhill into the water. I watched a large male slow-gallop down the beach, rippling its thick weight across the sand. Its insides seemed to be moving more slowly than its skin. Most of the seals seemed content to lie asleep on the sand, dreaming their slate-gray dreams.

body and rotate them in a wringing-of-the-hands movement. They don't get sunburned. They don't pass out from lying for many hours with their heads downhill. They do have hips, but narrow ones, and they sometimes cross their rear flippers, play patty-cake, or make praying-hands of

As the days passed, we often visited the little islands of French Frigate Shoals, and we were happy about all the monk seals we had seen, doctored (sometimes), and looked after. At last it was time for Bill and me to leave. We had heard a rumor that there were some more monk seals living near a tiny island a plane ride away, and we wanted to see if that was true, since so few monk seals remain. So we said good-bye to Gil, and all the monk seals of French Frigate Shoals, and flew back to Hawaii.

There we rented a boat, and after a three-hour sail through choppy waters, we arrived at a small channel between two islands, one with a towering mountain. We didn't see any monk seals at all. It was a hot day, so we decided to have lunch and then go snorkeling among the coral reefs. Bill and I put on our masks and fins and slipped underwater, enjoying the brightly colored fish and coral. I noticed a small bay and a sea cave, and I swam toward it to explore. Entering the bay, I swam through a

curtain of bubbles. Then I was in a quiet lagoon, with a sandy bottom about fifteen feet below. Ahead of me, a long gray shape maneuvered, just out of sight. Suddenly it turned, came closer, and stopped six feet in front of me. Staring me straight in the face was a large monk seal with black eyes and thick whiskers. Heaven only knows what was going through its mind! Eying me carefully, it dived underneath me, rolling over as it did, came up behind me, eyed me again, and swung to my right.

Two more seals appeared from behind the curtain of bubbles. They were rolling tightly together, chasing and playing. Occasionally they surfaced and *baah*ed loudly at one another. Then the female would dart away and the male would join her as they glided and spun. Bubbles trailed from them like comet tails. I saw them mating right below me, and I tried to watch very carefully, and remember every little thing, because no one had ever seen that before up close like this, and I wasn't sure anyone would have the chance to again.

◄ *A male monk seal pursues a mating partner.*

Night would soon be falling, and it was a long journey home best done in the daylight, so, reluctant but happy, I finned back to the boat. What an array of monk seals I had seen! Back at the boat, I told Bill everything I had seen, and he told me everything he had seen. We felt rich and happy. It had been a great visit. I had hoped I might catch a glimpse of monk seals in the wild, but I had no idea I would see so many, and be privy to their intimate behaviors. I find studying rare, beautiful, endangered animals great fun, but also a gift, a sacred duty, and a privilege. As we sailed away, we saw two seals swiveling tightly together among the coral. Over and over they rolled, spiraling gracefully through the water. Then we passed a mother seal, lying on the rocks rimming the lagoon, napping peacefully near her pup. After a while, the island grew tiny behind us, and the shining monk seals disappeared into their kingdom by the sea.

INDEX

Text copyright © 1995 by Diane Ackerman
Photographs copyright © 1991 by Bill Curtsinger
Map on page 8 copyright © 1995 by Gaylord Welker
Illustration on page 19 copyright © 1995
by Suzanne Barnes

Parts of this book first appeared in a different version
in National Geographic.

Published by Crown Publishers, Inc.,
a Random House company, 201 East 50th Street,
New York, New York 10022.

CROWN is a trademark of Crown Publishers, Inc.
Manufactured in Hong Kong

Library of Congress Cataloging-in-Publication Data
Ackerman, Diane.
Monk seal hideaway / by Diane Ackerman ;
photographs by Bill Curtsinger.
p. cm.
1. Hawaiian monk seal—Juvenile literature.
[1. Monk seals. 2. Seals. 3. Endangered species.
4. Rare animals.]
I. Curtsinger, Bill, 1946– ill. II. Title.
QL737.P64134   1995
599.74'8—dc20   94-7925
ISBN 0-517-59673-3 (trade)
     0-517-59674-1 (lib. bdg.)
10 9 8 7 6 5 4 3 2 1
First Edition